ANIMAL SAFARI

Jaguars

by Margo Gates

BELLWETHER MEDIA • MINNEAPOLIS, MN

Note to Librarians, Teachers, and Parents:

Blastoff! Readers are carefully developed by literacy experts and combine standards-based content with developmentally appropriate text.

Level 1 provides the most support through repetition of high-frequency words, light text, predictable sentence patterns, and strong visual support.

Level 2 offers early readers a bit more challenge through varied simple sentences, increased text load, and less repetition of high-frequency words.

Level 3 advances early-fluent readers toward fluency through increased text and concept load, less reliance on visuals, longer sentences, and more literary language.

Level 4 builds reading stamina by providing more text per page, increased use of punctuation, greater variation in sentence patterns, and increasingly challenging vocabulary.

Level 5 encourages children to move from "learning to read" to "reading to learn" by providing even more text, varied writing styles, and less familiar topics.

Whichever book is right for your reader, Blastoff! Readers are the perfect books to build confidence and encourage a love of reading that will last a lifetime!

This edition first published in 2014 by Bellwether Media, Inc.

Library of Congress Cataloging-in-Publication Data

Gates, Margo.
Jaguars / by Margo Gates.
p. cm. – (Blastoff! readers. Animal safari)
Summary: "Developed by literacy experts for students in kindergarten through grade three, this book introduces jaguars to young readers through leveled text and related photos"– Provided by publisher.
Audience: K to grade 3.
Includes bibliographical references and index.
ISBN 978-1-60014-911-5 (hardcover : alk. paper)
1. Jaguar–Juvenile literature. I. Title. II. Series: Blastoff! readers. 1, Animal safari.
QL737.C23G38 2014
599.75'5–dc23

2013000886

Printed in the United States of America, North Mankato, MN.

Contents

What Are Jaguars?

Jaguars are **big cats**. They have spots called **rosettes**.

Where Jaguars Live

Jaguars live in grasslands, forests, and **swamps**.

Some live in
rain forests.
They have
dark coats.

Hunting

Jaguars learn to hunt at a young age. Their mothers teach them.

They swim to hunt for fish, turtles, and caimans.

Jaguars **stalk** deer and capybaras on land. They hide behind branches and tall grass.

They also wait for **prey** in trees. Then they **pounce**.

Jaguars have strong **jaws** and sharp teeth. They can kill prey with one bite.

Then they drag their kill to a safe spot. They hide it from other **predators**. It is all yours, jaguar!

Glossary

big cats—large wild cats; lions, tigers, leopards, and jaguars are all big cats.

jaws—the bones that form the mouth of an animal

pounce—to leap on top of something

predators—animals that hunt other animals for food

prey—animals that are hunted by other animals for food

rain forests—warm, wet forests that get a lot of rain

rosettes—spots on a jaguar's coat; rosettes are shaped like roses.

stalk—to secretly follow

swamps—wetlands with trees and other plants

To Learn More

AT THE LIBRARY

Ganeri, Anita. *Jaguar*. Chicago, Ill.: Heinemann Library, 2011.

Guidone, Julie. *Jaguars*. New York, N.Y.: Gareth Stevens Pub., 2009.

Tourville, Amanda Doering. *A Jaguar Grows Up*. Minneapolis, Minn.: Picture Window Books, 2007.

ON THE WEB

Learning more about jaguars is as easy as 1, 2, 3.

1. Go to www.factsurfer.com.
2. Enter "jaguars" into the search box.
3. Click the "Surf" button and you will see a list of related Web sites.

With factsurfer.com, finding more information is just a click away.

Index

The images in this book are reproduced through the courtesy of: Chinawds, front cover; Rechitan Sorin, p. 5; Matt Gibson, pp. 7, 9; Antonio Jorge Nunes, p. 7 (left); Ivalin, p. 7 (middle); M Reel, p. 7 (right); Gerard Lacz/ Age Fotostock/ SuperStock, p. 11; Patrick Fagot/ Biosphoto, p. 13; Nantawat Chotsuwan, p. 13 (left); Kippy Spilker, p. 13 (middle); Ammit Jack, p. 13 (right); Pablo Hidalgo, p. 15; Eduardo Rivero, p. 15 (left); Vadim Petrakov, p. 15 (right); Eraldo Peres/ AP Images, p. 17; Thomas Marent/ Ardea.com, p. 19; Nick Garbutt/ Nature Picture Library, p. 21.